COUNTRY LIVING

decorating
with
candles

ACCENTS FOR EVERY ROOM

D1370419

COUNTRY LIVING

decorating with candles

ACCENTS FOR EVERY ROOM

by **MARIA RICAPITO**

photography by **KEITH SCOTT MORTON**

styling by **INGRID LEESS**

foreword by **NANCY MERNIT SORIANO**

HEARST BOOKS
A DIVISION OF STERLING PUBLISHING CO., INC.
NEW YORK

Copyright © 2000 by Hearst Communications, Inc.

For Country Living
Editor-in-Chief, Nancy Mernit Soriano
Deputy Editor, Lawrence A. Bilotti
Design Director, Susan M. Netzel

Produced by Smallwood and Stewart, Inc., New York City
Art Director: Debra Sfetsios

The Library of Congress has catalogued the hardcover edition as follows:
Country living decorating with candles.
          p. cm.
Includes index.
ISBN 0-688-17502-3
1. Candles in interior decoration. I. Country living (New York, N.Y.) II. Title:
Decorating with candles
NK2115.5.C35C68 2000
747'.92—dc21   99-36437

10 9 8 7 6 5 4 3 2 1

First Paperback Edition 2005
Published by Hearst Books
A Division of Sterling Publishing Co., Inc.
387 Park Avenue South, New York, NY 10016

Photography on pages 12, 13, 33, 40, 41, 45, 48, 49, 52, 53, 58, 61, 66, 68, 69, 70, 72,
73, 76, 79, 80, 81, 82, 85, 86, 87, 88, 91, 92, 97, 98, 105, 112, styled by the editors of
Country Living.

Cover photographs by Keith Scott Morton

Country Living is a trademark owned by Hearst Magazines Property, Inc., in USA,
and Hearst Communications, Inc., in Canada. Hearst Books is a trademark owned by
Hearst Communications, Inc.

www.countryliving.com

Distributed in Canada by Sterling Publishing
c/o Canadian Manda Group, 165 Dufferin Street
Toronto, Ontario, Canada M6K 3H6

Distributed in Australia by Capricorn Link (Australia) Pty. Ltd.
P.O. Box 704, Windsor, NSW 2756 Australia

Printed in China

ISBN 1-58816-443-8

table of **contents**

foreword

THERE IS SOMETHING TRULY WONDERFUL ABOUT candlelight. It adds atmosphere and warmth to a room, creates intimacy and romance at the dinner table, promotes rest and relaxation in the bath, and brings a magical glow to the garden at night. For centuries, candles have also played an important role as signifiers of tradition, from symbols of religion to signs of friendship, celebration, and life.

At *Country Living*, candles have always been an important part of the way we decorate our homes. As an ever-changing source of illumination, candlelight offers an emotional appeal that artificial light lacks. It can transform a room—and our moods—more quickly than any other decorating tool. And the abundance and diversity of candles today make them readily accessible to everyone.

In this book, we share creative ways to use candles and the qualities of candlelight throughout the house—from day-to-day enjoyment to special occasions and holidays. We hope you will take pleasure in lighting candles, as a way to add beauty and warmth to your home . . . and to your life.

—NANCY MERNIT SORIANO

Editor-in-Chief

introduction

IN THE NOT-SO-DISTANT PAST, CANDLES ILLUMINATED our lives and our homes, and shaped both. We lived by the rhythms of the changing light of the day: The seasons, our activities, and even the colors and decor of our rooms were shaped by the value of candlelight. Today, light is not as precious as it once was, and perhaps for that reason we are less sensitive to its properties and its moods. Candles in our homes remind us of the essential qualities of light and of its profound emotional power.

This is a book about using candle power within your home: to bring a room to life, to highlight a favorite collection, or to disguise an unattractive corner. In the following pages we show how to decorate with candles in ways that are vibrant and energetic or subdued and intimate; to add energy to a setting or imbue it with serenity.

Candles have always inspired warmth, friendliness, hope, and guidance. Like its subject, we trust this book, too, is inspirational. Use the ideas, both grand and humble, to make your home as a beautiful, dazzling reflection of you.

candles in the home

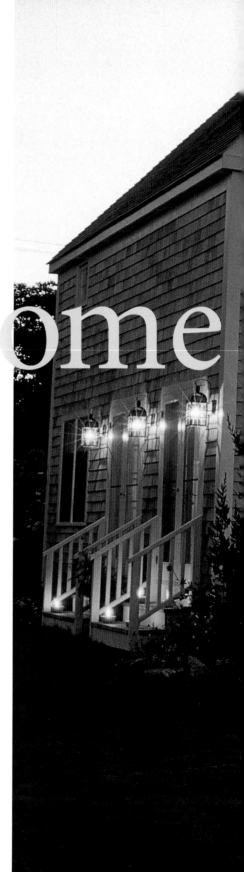

Two ivory-colored pillars in dark-bodied holders, surrounded by fresh fruit and flowers, look pretty lit or unlit (ABOVE). Candlelight is alluring, whether it is indoors or out (RIGHT). A candle in the window and a well-lit doorway have long been symbols of welcome to friends and strangers alike.

THE ENCHANTMENT OF CANDLELIGHT LIES IN ITS unique ability to transform even the most ordinary surroundings into an intimate world of comfort, charm, and sometimes even mystery and romance. In the home, a candle's welcoming glow draws us inside, then invites us to linger in the aura of a simpler time, when firelight was the only source of illumination and warmth.

A hallway illuminated with several sconces is prettier than one lit with a harsh electric light. Choose traditional brass sconces, or try sleek contemporary ones. Vary the height of the sconces to soften the light even more and dramatize the perspective of the space.

Today, the soft tones candles cast create atmosphere and mood in home decorating schemes and provide a restful break from our often overlit world. On a front walk, candelarias are beacons of welcome; in entryways, flickering candles give visitors the impression of warmth; on a dining table, slender tapers encourage quiet, substantive conversation; at bedside, perfumed candles promise romance and peaceful dreams. Regardless of the room, a grouping of candles fills the space with gentle, golden light and rich, deep shadows.

The successful use of candles inside and outside the home depends on where they are placed and how they are designed. As the sole light source, a profusion of candles will bathe a room in a soft light, ideal for cozy socializing and private talks. But if direct attention to a favorite object or interesting architectural feature is needed, candles can be combined, sometimes with other ambient light sources, to create a focal point.

The pleasure of candlelight should be enjoyed often. Allow the simple purity and traditional beauty of candles to add grace notes to your life every day.

ENTRYWAYS

First impressions of your home are made in the entrance hall, reserved for welcoming guests and putting strangers at their ease. Through the imaginative use

I n many homes, the hallways share space with a staircase. Emphasize the architectural interest of stairs with lighting. However, to ensure safety, protect the candles by enclosing them in pretty lanterns or hurricanes.

of candlelight, these sometimes cramped spaces can be made to establish a friendly and welcoming atmosphere. When you enter from outdoors, candlelight is much easier on the eyes than the light from a bright electrical fixture. If necessary, gentle candlelight can be supplemented with a low-wattage overhead light.

Sconces are a logical choice for a vestibule, since they take up only a small amount of wall space. Fixtures with mirrored or brightly polished metal backings will multiply the amount of light in an entryway, even when the candles are not lit. As a safety precaution, install sconces so that the candles cannot be caught in drafts when exterior doors are opened and closed. Keeping lit candles out of drafts will also hold soot to a minimum. Finally, never leave lit candles in an entranceway unattended for long periods.

DECORATING ENTRYWAYS WITH CANDLES

✷

✷ **SET A MOOD:** Just one lightly scented candle on a side table will establish an inviting atmosphere for guests.

✷ **MIX STYLES:** Instead of the traditional pair of sconces, line an entry hall with a collection of sconces of mixed styles. Unify the look with candles of the same color and style.

✷ **ADD INTEREST:** Make the back door as welcoming as the front. Hang a simple brass sconce nearby and keep a candle lit when guests are expected.

✷ **GUIDE GUESTS:** Votives on a staircase or along a dark hallway lead visitors into your home.

CONSIDER FOUND OBJECTS

Inspiration for turning ordinary objects into candleholders is everywhere. Garage sales and flea markets are great places to pick up inexpensive items. Here are a few ideas:

✺ **KITCHENWARE:** Look for candy molds, biscuit tins, and pudding cups; a muffin pan will hold several votives as a centerpiece.

✺ **MISMATCHED CHINA:** Raid cupboards for old cake stands, glass dessert bowls, wine coasters, and saucers or teacups for votives or pillars.

✺ **GARDEN PLANTERS:** Check the potting shed for flowerpots and planters that can be resurrected as candleholders.

T*he garden is bursting with ideas for holders in all shapes and sizes. Terra-cotta pots just need to be scrubbed and filled with big pillars, then massed on a sideboard with greens.*

A small foyer table is also an excellent place for a candle arrangement. It could offer a place of honor for a pair of prized heirloom candlesticks protected under hurricanes or a collection of pillars grouped on a wooden or tole tray. Throughout the year, add seasonal flowers and greens to the table and even to sconces to extend the hospitality of your home to everyone who arrives.

LIVING ROOMS

After the foyer, the living room is often the first room that guests enter. Here much is revealed about the hosts, including their hobbies and interests, and their attitudes, toward others and toward life. The candle has always served as a symbol of hospitality and warmth, and making candlelight an integral part of the living room is an important part of living well.

In some homes, the living room is a formal area,

*C*andles placed in shiny galvanized pails, brass lanterns, or decorative tin votives will enhance their gleam and bring an empty hearth to life.

conceived in the manner of the old-fashioned parlor as a place to entertain special guests. If the living room is rarely occupied, it usually has been decorated more formally and may feature favorite possessions such as antique porcelain, old family paintings, and heirloom rugs.

In other homes, the living room is precisely that—a room for living. It is a casual, multifunctional space where family members meet to watch television, read, play games, and talk.

Some homes are elaborate enough to have both a formal room for special occasions and a casual space, either a family room or great room, for everyday family life. The great room, the notion of which harks back to Colonial days, is often built next to—or, in some cases, is even part of—the kitchen. In many homes, most family meals are served there rather than in a formal dining room.

CANDLELIT FIREPLACES

During warmer weather, turn your empty fireplace into an attractive focal point in the room with a flickering still life of lit candles:

✸ **MIX** pillar candles of varying heights and widths, including several votives. Arrange small candles in the front and larger ones toward the back and the sides.

✸ **USE** upturned flowerpots, bricks, a small bench, or children's blocks to vary the height of the candles and enhance the play of the flames.

✸ **COMBINE** candleholders including lanterns, glass jars, hurricanes, tin cans or pails with cutout designs, and porcelain saucers to create variety and interest.

O ld-fashioned birdcages (ABOVE) add interest to the plainest pillar candle and can be found in antiques shops and flea markets. Look for cages with removable bases, and set the candle on a clear glass saucer to catch drips. With a wooden birdcage, make sure the flame does not burn too closely to the top and sides of the cage.

An antique stepladder or library steps make an excellent place to display a mix off ornately carved and molded candles (OPPOSITE).

Living Room Lighting

Regardless of whether a living room is formal or casual, it can be enhanced with creative candlelight. What's more, living rooms need several different types of light sources to accommodate the activities that take place in them. Although candlelight is far prettier and more flattering than electric light, most people require stronger light to read, sew, and do other activities that require sharp eyes.

Soft ambient lighting from sconces or chandeliers and one or two floor or table lamps will generate a pleasing background and sufficient task light for most activities. This light can be augmented with individual candles or groupings of candles elsewhere in the room. A mix of elegant tapers in interesting candlesticks set on a side table, for example, can provide as much light as a small lamp and create a feeling of warmth no electric fixture could ever generate.

Formal or Informal Decorating

For a formal living room, antique silver candlesticks or elaborate candelabra arranged on a dark wood side table achieve an harmonious effect. A cluster of crystal candlesticks, of various sizes and shapes and alight with pure white tapers, also creates an accent more suitable to a formal setting.

Etched glass makes an especially lovely candleholder. The fronds tucked under these pillar candles mirror the ferns etched on the glass containers.

In a casual living room, both candles and candlesticks can afford to be more eclectic. Two or three dark red pillars set inside plain hurricane lamps on a rustic coffee table are appropriate. Or, a cluster of small pillars on a shallow spongeware bowl may be all that is necessary.

Shared Elements

All living rooms share certain elements that can be enhanced by candlelight. A fireplace with a mantel, for example, serves as a focal point. In a formal living room, festooning a Federal-style mantel with cream-colored pillars and votives in glass lamps will set up a dazzling display of light sufficient to rival the charm of an 18th-century salon. In a less formal family room, arranging turquoise-colored tapers in tin or pounded-silver candlesticks on the mantle of a stone fireplace achieves an artistic yet homey feel.

SEASONAL CANDLES

✿

Embellish candles with flowers and plants that mirror the seasons:

✿ **SPRING:** Combine potted bulbs such as daffodils, tulips, dog's tooth violets, crocus, and hyacinths with pastel-colored candles in shades of yellow, pink, pale blue, or lavender.

✿ **SUMMER:** Go for chunky white pillars set among bunches of pink or blue hydrangeas in rustic baskets.

✿ **FALL:** Arrange candles in autumnal hues with a basket of pinecones, gourds, bittersweet, ivy, and, of course, autumn leaves.

✿ **WINTER:** Combine flats of forced paperwhite bulbs with snowy white votives nestled in sphagnum moss.

If the fireplace in question is in the living room of a casual beach house, it might be fun to arrange children's beach pails on the hearth, filled with sand— or better still, sea glass—holding a mix of pillar candles. The whole display could be set off with driftwood, shells, stones, and perhaps even an old watering can or florist's bucket brimming with roadside flowers or summer daisies.

A formal living room and a homey great room each may each contain family collections that can be beautifully illuminated with candlelight, especially if that collection will, in turn, reflect the flickering light. Low white tapers in elegant crystal holders, for example, might be the perfect choice to illuminate a prized collection of antique mercury glass or silver displayed in a formal living room. Or, several lit votives may be all that is needed to bring a grouping of Victorian wine glasses or vintage Christmas ornaments to life.

Most of all, formal and the casual living rooms share people. In both spaces, family and friends will meet to talk and share the pleasures of life. Warm candlelight can enhance that experience and enrich the mood. Very often, the more candles that light up a room, the more animated and festive the room will seem to the inhabitants. (Long before electric lighting, the "specialness" of an occasion—and the wealth of the

*C*andlelight can be enhanced in dozens of ways. Placing candles in front of a reflective surface, like these Edwardian mirrored sconces, is always successful and always pretty. Positioning shiny or mirrored pieces so that they reflect daylight also enhances the illumination in a room. For safety, if lit candles are placed near windows, curtains should be tied back securely.

erra-cotta pots aren't the only garden containers that can come indoors for candles. An iron garden urn filled with florist's moss is a charming holder for a pillar candle (ABOVE). Experiment to find the candle size that looks best and fits with your container. When arranging lit candles on top of a tall armoire (OPPOSITE), place them far from the ceiling so soot will not mar the paint.

host—dictated the number of candles used to illuminate the party and the length of time the candles were allowed to burn.) Increase your candlepower by placing candles next to a mirror, window, polished tiles, or other shiny surfaces. Sconces, particularly, seem brighter when backed with silver or brass. Even high–gloss paint on the walls will multiply the light. The effect in a room lit with scores of candles is one of lightness, happiness, and joy.

Conversely, by subduing the candlelight, a mood of intrigue and romance can be created. Everyone knows a pair of slim tapers casting a soft light will instantly add to the intimacy of an occasion.

DINING ROOMS

Candlelight makes an event out of a meal. Its warmth enhances, its gentleness softens, and the muted, ever-changing light provides continuing but unobtrusive interest to the room. No dining room or dining table is dressed for guests without the presence of candles.

Chandeliers

Whether its design is Colonial or fishing-lodge rustic, a chandelier is an obvious light source for a dining table, and the nature and amount of light it supplies set the mood for the room.

*C*handeliers are easy to decorate for Sunday suppers and formal parties. Ivy woven onto chandelier arms is an attractive addition that will stay fresh through an evening meal.

If the chandelier is electric, install a dimmer switch so that the brighter light can be muted to suit the mood of the occasion. Add sconces to the dining room walls and position candles around the room. Utilize reflective surfaces such as polished metals, china, crystal, windows, and mirrors to accentuate the play of candlelight on the other elements in the room. Turn down lighting in the adjoining rooms while you are at table to keep the atmosphere tranquil and serene.

If you want to add a candle chandelier over the table in the dining area and can't find one in a style you like, search flea markets for old electrified fixtures. Simply remove the wiring and replace the cardboard candle sleeves with wax tapers. Be sure to add drip trays or bobeches under the candle cups or use non–drip candles. Hang your new creation by its chain from the

FIVE CANDLE CENTERPIECES

🌼 **MAKE A CANDELABRA** by placing a glass cake stand in the center of the table, with votives around the rim and a low round pillar in the center.

🌼 **PLACE SIMPLE VOTIVES** on plain white servers to illuminate each setting.

🌼 **USE PILLARS** of various heights in colors to match an arrangement of fruit or vegetables—a bowl of lemons with pale lemon-colored candles, for example, or pears with candles in earth tones.

🌼 **LINE A TRAY** with sphagnum moss and place votives on the moss.

🌼 **STAND A LINE** of low pillars on a reflecting surface, such as a silver tray or long mirror, in the center of the table.

A Colonial country room is lit with candles in the most classic manner. Single tapers are centered in each window, a simple chandelier lights the dining area, and two dipped candles in pewter candlesticks illuminate the table. A lovely pewter sconce decorates the wall over the serving dresser, while oil lamps add extra light to the scene.

ceiling, high enough so guests will not bump their heads on it but low enough to envelop the table and its occupants with soft light.

Also, consider decorating your chandelier on special occasions and holidays. For a formal party, weave strings of glass beads or wire garlands of fresh or dried flowers into the arms. At Christmas, hang evergreens, ivy, gingerbread men, or treasured ornaments with wire or tie them on with satin ribbon.

Candles on the Table

Candles are as important on the table as they are in chandeliers or sconces. They bring not only light but a sense of hospitality and intimacy that can even make the food seem more special.

*I*ndoors or outdoors, or in a hybrid of both (ABOVE), even the most unique setting can benefit from a few well-placed candles. Here, an old barn remade into a dining room has walls covered in sheets of ivy, which took a decade to grow. The table glows with a few pillar candles in striking oversized holders.

A wrought-iron chandelier fitted with chunky-yet-elegant pillars casts a flattering light over a dinner table (OPPOSITE). Strings of crystal beads contribute a touch of whimsy to the chandelier.

Flowers and greenery naturally complement the candles' stately grace. Arrange them together, picking up the colors of flowers with the hues of candles. When combining candles and flowers, check that the arrangement is a size that allows diners to speak comfortably with one another across the table without having to lean to one side to look around the centerpiece. In winter, use evergreen boughs as a bed for pillars and votives, as a wreath around the base of a candle or candleholder, or in a tabletop arrangement with tapers.

If food is being served from a sideboard or buffet, concentrate plenty of candlelight in that area as well.

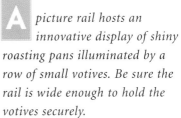 picture rail hosts an innovative display of shiny roasting pans illuminated by a row of small votives. Be sure the rail is wide enough to hold the votives securely.

Ceramic and glass containers may be adapted as candleholders, but they can shatter. The top opening should be wider or just barely smaller than the base to allow heat to escape. A little water or sand inside the container can help dissipate the heat. Do a test run: Light the candle inside the holder, and after a minute, hold the back of your hand near the side of the container. If it feels hot after such a short time, it's probably not a good choice, as it might crack.

Candelabra, tapers under hurricane lamps, or an assemblage of pillars will supply enough light for guests to appreciate the display and for the host to serve.

Candles in any dining area should not do battle with the delicious aromas of the food. For most situations, reserve scented candles for other rooms.

KITCHENS

Ironically, we somehow forget that the kitchen is a marvelous room to illuminate with candlelight. For thousands of years, the kitchen fire was the place where food was cooked. With the invention of electric and gas stoves, the notion of the kitchen flame was forgotten. But it's well worth reconsidering.

Candlelight is not efficient to work by in the kitchen, but its powers to conceal and romanticize come into play once the meal has been prepared. If your kitchen is visible to guests, pots and any messy cleanup can be hidden from view just by lighting one or two candles to illuminate food preparation areas. Turn off the kitchen fixtures and light a few pillar candles just before serving. The candles will provide an attractive glow and will guide you as you serve your guests.

If you eat in the kitchen every day, place two or three container candles on the table. Just before serving food, turn off the electrical lights, and dine by candlelight.

Clear glass vases and bowls have been filled with bright yellow floating votives as centerpieces for an outdoor party. A few lemons bobbing in the water continue the citrusy theme and keep the candles from bumping into each other and overturning. The whole effect is light, airy, and utterly unique.

An unexpected variation on
the classic table setting of
twin candlesticks uses a bouquet
of thick multi-wick pillars flanked
by elegant, matched topiaries
(LEFT). Stately white candles and
fine silver on a sideboard create
an intimate and elegant mood for
a small dinner party (ABOVE).

A mix of candles brightens an inviting breakfast in bed. Varying widths of lavender ribbon unite the different candles.

BEDROOMS

Your bedroom should be a place of repose, where comfort reigns and the lighting surrounds you in softness, like being wrapped in a familiar quilt. Not that long ago, we made our way to bed each night by candlelight, carefully cupping the flame against drafts. Now we shut off the electric lights along the way, a process that is often more jarring than tranquil. Instead, it is far more soothing to end the day by the gentle flicker of candlelight.

Candles in soft colors—white, neutrals, or pastels—coordinate well with the natural textures and tones of a country bedroom. Here is a good place to give in to the appeal of scented candles and candles decorated with ribbons and pressed flowers.

If you prefer a single source of candlelight at your bedside, group pillars or tapers of differing heights on a side table, or arrange several votives on a delicate platter. A small punched-tin lantern makes a delightful decorative accent; the light patterns coming through the

SCENTS & SENSIBILITY

Burning perfume and essential oils is a timeless way to add fragrance to the bedroom. The easiest method is simply to light a scented candle. But you can also customize the scent by using a porcelain vaporizer. Just place a lit votive in the base, and add a drop or two of the cologne or essential oil you like best to the bowl. Soon the entire room will be filled with your favorite fragrance.

pierced holes are charming. One short candlestick or a small candelabra can be equally pleasing. Place the candle arrangement close to the bed so you can extinguish them without having to get up.

Sometimes you aren't ready for sleep, but just want a little relaxation. Positioning a candle in front of the mirror on the dresser or scattering individual votives on shelves, windowsills, and other flat surfaces will cast a serene glow over the whole room. To concentrate the light in one area, arrange candles on a blanket chest, a tray, or a footstool.

Keep candles out of drafts and away from flammable fabrics and drapes and never, never fall asleep without extinguishing all candles. In the bedroom, floating candles are a good option, as is grounding votives in sand. If you should fall asleep before extinguishing them, the water or sand will do it for you.

BATHROOMS

Casting a gentle glow that bounces off reflecting tile surfaces, candlelight seems to belong in the bathroom. After all, what good is a relaxing soak in the bath if you're surrounded by harsh lighting?

For a room so intimate, the bathroom often has a stark and unfriendly atmosphere, hardly conducive to relaxing. By introducing a gentle play of light and shadow

F ormal candlesticks (ABOVE) can spell a special occasion even in the bathroom. An exotic tableau is created with Polynesian candles, straw slippers, and plush towels (OPPOSITE). The flames draw the eye upward from the floor over every piece of the candle collection. To lend a touch of nature to candles in the bathroom, wrap big leaves or vines from the garden around them and tie with a long piece of grass (or raffia from a craft store). Try candles scented with natural aromas such as fresh-cut grass, herbs, pine, or flowers.

AROMATHERAPY FOR THE BATH

Essential oils and scents particularly suited for relaxing in the tub include:

EUCALYPTUS—The clean aroma helps ease muscle aches and pains and relieve head colds.

JASMINE—The fruity, flowery fragrance helps reduce stress and dispel depression. It is also considered to be an aphrodisiac.

JUNIPER—The intense pine-needle scent of juniper is both invigorating and comforting.

LAVENDER—The distinctive flowery scent of lavender soothes, calms, and brings a sense of well-being.

PEPPERMINT—With its invigorating aroma, peppermint makes a good pick-me-up when energy is flagging and the day is not quite done.

ROSE—The heady richness of the rose is one of the most universally appealing scents. It always calms the soul, clears the mind, and lightens the heart.

A *beachcomer shows off her finds by using shells as candle molds, bringing the unmistakable aura of the seaside to a bathroom.*

that softens hard edges and establishes a cozy feel, candlelight will transform the room immediately.

Candles in the bathroom are about more than just decoration. Soaking in a tub by candlelight is the perfect way to restore one's balance at the end of a long day. Scented candles are a good choice for the bathroom, where their delightful fragrance freshens the air and their mood-enhancing qualities can be enjoyed bathside without distractions. Many tubs have wide, flat corners that can hold a candle, or even a rim deep enough to ring with pillars. Or, bring in a small bench or low, flat-topped stool and call it into service as a candle stand. If there is shelf or vanity space, it can hold one or more candles in addition to pretty soaps or other decorative items. A windowsill or tile ledge invites a montage of pillars or votives.

candles
outdoors

An elegant candelabra, a pair of sterling silver candlesticks, and vintage flatware brought into the garden create a very special outdoor dinner party (ABOVE AND RIGHT). Votives in simple glass holders make the whole table glisten. Even the cherub has a candle to help illuminate the gathering.

THROUGHOUT THE YEAR, THE FLICKERING light of candles can transform the landscape around your home, illuminating the darkness while preserving the mystery of the night. As accent lighting in the garden or backyard and on the porch or patio, candles make it possible to enjoy the pleasure of being outdoors long past nightfall and still appreciate the stars.

Before electricity was brought outdoors, alfresco lighting was provided by candle lamps, which featured glass globes to protect the flame, much like the chimneys on oil lamps. Other styles boasted tin shades. Many of these lamps also had handles, which allowed the lantern to be hung or carried where needed.

Sconces too were often adapted for outside use, designed with three sides that protected the candle. In this way, a permanent night light could be left on the porch when a guest or family member was expected home after dark.

Today there are so many ways to utilize candles outdoors: as miniature chandeliers hanging from tree branches; as luminarias glowing around a pool or serving as guiding lights along paths; in glass votive jars lining the railings of the porch, deck, or gazebo.

To be an effective lighting source outdoors, candles need only a place to stand or hang safely, perhaps with a wind screen to foil passing breezes. Since the 19th century, when it was discovered that adding the fatty acid stearin to tallow made candles harder and lengthened their burn time, advances in the manufacture of wicks and commercial paraffin have made it possible to produce long-burning candles exclusively for outdoor use. Some torches and citronella-oil candles can burn cheerfully for three hours or more, depending on the wind.

C andles in glass containers are easy-to-use decorating tools, especially outdoors, because they are stable and protected from breezes.

*C*andles outdoors can be as casual or as romantic as they are inside. Try massing a dozen or more votives on a high-sided tray (ABOVE), or line a porch with container candles (OPPOSITE) to create a strong, luminous glow, bright enough to illuminate any social gathering.

ALL WELCOME

One of the primary functions of candles outdoors is to project a warm, comforting welcome. On the lawn, along the front path, and on the porch or stairs, candles serve as decorative beacons of light to guide you safely from the street to the door.

Weary travelers treading the dusty country lanes of long ago knew that a house with a candle in the window meant that a friendly welcome and the warmth of a fire awaited them inside. The same feeling of welcome can be extended today to anyone approaching your home, when he or she is greeted from the road with an outdoor display of candlelight.

To line a walkway with glowing luminarias, choose white paper bags for a cleaner light, colored or patterned bags for a party atmosphere. If you like, cut designs in the sides of the bags so the flame can glow more brightly through the openings. If you wish the design to be clearly lit by the candle, then the luminaria should be opaque (black kraft paper is good). Alternatively, stencil your

CANDLE PLACECARDS

✸ **WRITE** each guest's name with glass paint on individual glass votive holders.

✸ **ATTACH** a votive with floral clay to a small flat stone painted with a guest's initials. The stones will also hold down napkins.

✸ **PAINT** a guest's name on the side of a miniature terra-cotta flowerpot. Tie raffia or a ribbon bow under the rim. Set the votive on some sphagnum moss inside the pot.

✸ **CUT** the tops from firm fruits and vegetables, such as apples, oranges, pomegranates, miniature pumpkins, and gourds. With an apple corer or melon baller, hollow out the flesh, then insert a votive. With a metallic marker, write each guest's name on a leaf. Place a fruit or vegetable votive on top so the name shows.

F or outdoor entertaining, place glass hurricane shades over candleholders to keep the candle flames alight.

designs onto the bag in black ink.

For a more formal (and all-seasons) approach, choose hanging lanterns for your welcoming lights. Reproductions of old-fashioned carriage lamps as well as contemporary decorative leaded-glass or punched-tin lanterns are readily available in candle and gift shops. Hang a pair of lanterns on each side of your front door, for example, or line several up the front steps and then cluster two or three more on the porch. To throw even more light, hang lanterns with plant hooks from a fence to outline the driveway or to border the front walk. When lanterns are raised off the ground, their light is more diffused, illuminating a larger area than when they are at ground level. If you have a wonderful tree or a striking bush in your front yard, highlight it with many small votives set in glass holders along the base, or hang miniature lanterns from the branches.

Blue, purple, pink, and white flowers are combined with candles and candleholders of the same hues to create lush decorative touches for an elegant outdoor party (ABOVE AND RIGHT). Once the sun has gone down, the candles will enjoy center stage with the anemones and roses.

Bright blue votives line a deck railing while blue and white votives create a starlight effect on the early American dining table. Don't forget to light up a citronella candle (on the post).

ENTERTAINING

The guiding principle for lighting an outdoor party is to illuminate at least three areas: the specific party area, the general focal points of the yard, and the important party details. The more subtly you combine light with various kinds of sources on different levels, the more inviting the party will look.

First, lanterns, pillars, or torches define the specific party areas. For example, mark the paths from the street to the garden or the house to the backyard. Highlight the central party area and, with candlelight, show guests how to find the bar and buffet table or dining table. Establish boundaries or barriers to keep people from unwittingly straying into the herb garden or any other area that is off-limits.

Second, hurricane lamps, kerosene lamps, tin lanterns, or masses of votives illuminate the architectal

CITRONELLA SECRETS

※ **CITRONELLA** candles are infused with aromatic citronella oil, which possesses a distinctly pungent aroma. In addition to being an insect repellent, citronella is also a base for complex perfumes. Because of its association with insecticides, citronella is not often used in aromatherapy. However, it will combine well with more popular essential oil scents, and still repel bugs.

※ **WHEN MIXED WITH** eucalyptus essential oil, the fragrance of citronella will become invigorating; with lavender, soothing; with rose, it becomes sensual. Because it is related to lemongrass, citronella also combines beautifully with lemon, geranium, or rosemary to make a more pleasing scent.

U nder a dramatic rooftop
gazebo, nothing should
compete with the view. If you are
giving a party in such an exciting
environment, keep the color
scheme unified and basic—white
candles, white flowers, and white
linens, for example.

Tiny fishbowls become lanterns when dangled from a beach umbrella, aided by twists of wire around their rims. Fill the bowls with an inch or so of water, then add a votive or a floating candle. The water will keep the wax from sticking to the glass and hold the candle level. This trick works well in your own backyard. Instead of fishbowls, you might hang canning jars rigged with votives to the branches of a tree.

features of the house and yard. Outline the entrance to the house and any steps, so that guests have enough light to move around safely.

Hang a chandelier from an arch, pergola, or other romantic spot in the garden. Festoon a gazebo by lining votives around its floor, railings, and roof. Add a touch of elegance to a stone wall or brick barbecue by perching one or more candelabra on top.

Keep the perimeter around a pool well lit, whether or not swimming is on the agenda, both for safety and because the reflections of the candles in the water can truly be mesmerizing. As a romantic accent and for a memorable effect, float candles in the pool water. Floating candles will also add a charming shimmer to the humblest birdbath or pond.

Finally, illuminate the details of party traffic areas such as the buffet or dining tables and the bar. Group banks of pillars, tapers, and votives on the tables to shed light on the food and on the faces of fellow diners. Cluster pillars and tapers in holders.

THE BEACH

For a dusk-to-dark picnic at the beach, tuck several standard-sized tapers in your basket. As the sky darkens and bottles of wine or soda are emptied, fill them

SIMPLE BEACH CANDLEHOLDERS

❋

Here are a few ideas for making quick candleholders that are perfect for a beach house—inside or out.

❋ **SAND PAILS:** Turn children's metal sand pails into lanterns by filling them halfway with sand and inserting votives or short pillar candles. Set them on posts or tabletops.

❋ **SEASHELLS:** Recycle clam and oyster shells by soaking them in a mild bleach solution for at least an hour (scrub them, if necessary). Rinse and let them dry. Melt the base of a small votive by holding it over a flame, letting the wax drip into the shell, then press in the candle.

❋ **LOGS OR DRIFTWOOD:** Make simple rustic wood holders for low pillars from small logs, or create a driftwood candelabra by using molten wax to attach votives.

halfway with sand or pebbles, and insert a taper into each bottleneck (use only glass bottles). Or, evoke memories of childhood by packing along six or eight empty Mason or mayonnaise jars and turning them into informal lamps: Fill the jars with sand, sea glass, small shells, pebbles, glass marbles, or slightly dampened moss to stabilize the container in gusts of wind. Insert a votive or a pillar candle, light, and enjoy.

OUTDOORS EVERY DAY

It's not just guests who deserve the pleasure of dining outdoors by candlelight. An evening meal enjoyed alfresco is a perfect opportunity for the family to share time together. Conversation becomes easier, and even simple hamburgers will taste better by candlelight.

You don't need to exert much energy to achieve a lovely effect with candles. Line the railings of the porch, patio, or deck with votive holders. Hang lanterns from tree branches and place a few hurricane lamps over thick pillars here and there on the floor, on tree stumps or boulders. For the center of a picnic table, fill an empty aquarium with pillar candles of various sizes, or gang up a collection of old candlesticks.

Sitting outside at the end of a long summer day can be restorative to body and soul. And candlelight, with the gentle chiaroscuro it creates, is inherently calming. Settling into an Adirondack chair, sipping a glass of wine or cup of tea, and gazing into a candle or two will provide just the right atmosphere for contemplation and relaxation.

OUTDOOR CANDLES IN WINTER

Summer is not the only time to decorate with candles outdoors. Winter can be gloomy, and sometimes made worse by gray skies. Set out lanterns to glitter over the frozen landscape or to spotlight the area leading to your door— as a quick and warming way to brighten cold, dark days and even darker nights. Line votives along porch railings and mass hurricanes over brightly colored pillars on the floor of the porch when expecting guests.

Making ice lanterns is great fun, an activity even children can enjoy. The result is a perfect combination of glistening ice and heartwarming candlelight.

A sunporch in winter
(LEFT) *may seem like
a contradiction in terms, but you
can light candles, curl up on the
sofa, and enjoy the pleasure of sun
glinting on snow. Lanterns from a
hardware store* **(ABOVE)** *keep
candles glowing in harsh weather.*

ce lanterns break the long, cold darkness of winter with a golden glow (ABOVE and OPPOSITE). *Place one or two outside the front door, or make several and line a walkway.*

MAKE ICE LANTERNS

One of the joys of winter, ice lanters are virtually free for the asking. In colder parts of the country, they are as common as snowfall, and steady brisk temperatures keep them glowing until spring. It's not necessary to wait for dark to light them; they are a beacon anytime.

✺ **FILL A PLASTIC** bucket about 14 inches deep and 7 inches in diameter with water to 2 inches from the top. Float a smaller container, about 3 inches deep and 4 inches in diameter, centered in the bucket. (The candles you plan to use should be slightly smaller than this container.) Freeze.

✺ **TO ADD FLOWERS,** herbs, leaves or berries, freeze them in stages, placing more material on top of each frozen layer.

✺ **FILL THE SMALL** container with warm water to loosen it, then remove it from the ice. Place the bucket in a warm-water bath to loosen the ice form, then slip it out of the bucket.

✺ **LINE THE INDENTATION** created by the small container with plastic wrap. Place a small pillar in the depression.

✺ **IF THE TEMPERATURE** outside is above freezing, the lanterns will last two or three hours after they are lit.

SNOWBALL LANTERNS

 Fill ordinary balloons with water and freeze (outdoors if cold enough). When frozen, pop the balloons and peel them off. Stack several ice balls to make an ice container.

 To make holes for the votives, slowly pour boiling water in the center of the ice container. Make the hole deep enough that the candle flame is at the surface of thelantern or the melting ice will extinguish the flame.

 Insert the candles in the holes and set the lanterns outside.

I nside an igloo of snowballs, a large candle casts its glow. The structure is built in stages and is doused with water after each stage to freeze it.

71

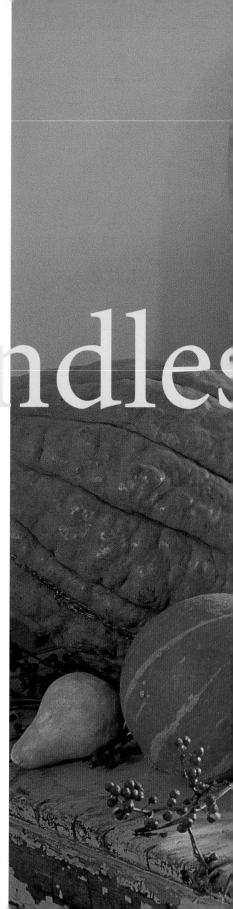

holidays
with candles

Clustered next to reflective silver balls, mercury glass vases, and crystal liqueur glasses several pillar candles create a festive look (ABOVE). Pumpkins, gourds, pears, and sprays of bittersweet lit by pillars on tall brass candlesticks decorate a Thanksgiving sideboard (RIGHT). The soft glow is enhanced by a mirror.

N O CELEBRATION IS COMPLETE WITHOUT candles. If a "candle season" exists, it begins at Halloween with jack-o'-lanterns and luminarias, and proceeds through to the sparkling tapers that make New Year's Eve special. For it is during the short days and long nights of late fall and winter that the warm, golden light cast by candles is most welcome throughout the home.

HALLOWEEN CANDLES

✺ **PLACE** a miniature orange pillar in the center of a small glass dish. Then fill the dish with multi-colored candy corn and pumpkins.

✺ **FEATURE ORANGE** or black tapers in a Halloween centerpiece. Put black tapers in wrought-iron candlesticks or pumpkin-colored tapers in crystal or brass candlesticks.

✺ **INSTEAD OF PUMPKINS**, look for gourds or winter squashes (butternut or hubbard, for example) to whittle into unusual luminarias.

✺ **TO WELCOME GUESTS**, carve the number of your house in a pumpkin, and place it near the driveway or mailbox. Light the candle every night.

*P*lacing a pumpkin luminara on each step of the staircase is a delightful way to decorate for Halloween. Try using pumpkins in different sizes and styles, including jack-o'-lanterns. Or keep the design consistent, and increase only the size of the pumpkins.

HALLOWEEN

Halloween, or the eve of All Saints' Day, is an old Celtic festival dating to the fifth century. It was believed that on the night of October 31st the spirit of the dead returned to their homes for just one night. In order to scare away evil spirits, country folk carved garish faces into hollowed-out turnips, placed candles inside, and put them outside their doors. In America, the pumpkin replaced the turnip, but the jack-o'-lantern continued to be an essential part of this ancient celebration.

Today, jack-o'-lanterns remain focal points for Halloween decorating. Instead of just one pumpkin, group several on a table, on a bed of colorful autumn leaves, and place tapers and votives in crystal holders among them to make the table glow.

THANKSGIVING

When the puritans gathered to give thanks for their successful first harvest, humble tallow candles lent a cheerful amber glow to the celebration. Decorations for this time of year should reflect the abundance of colors and textures of the autumn harvest. Although this holiday is about plenty, simplicity is the key to decorating.

Pile apples and pears into wooden bowls and troughs and flank them with fragrant beeswax tapers in candlesticks of verdigris metal or earthenware. Hollow pumpkins, squashes, and gourds to be used as luminarias, but instead of carving scary faces, try pretty repeat patterns of circles, stripes, or stars.

Use candles in vibrant autumn colors, such as yellows, golds, reds, and oranges, to add richness. Bring out toleware candlesticks and pair them with burgundy red candles, or tie lemon leaves to the bottom of yellow tapers with raffia and insert them into wooden bobbins. Place cream-colored pillars in a willow basket filled with pomegranates and pinecones.

Pillar candles are a good choice in areas where space is limited. Put one in a shallow redware bowl and add some spicy potpourri for a powder room vanity or hall table. Wrap a pillar with cinnamon sticks tied on with raffia and place it on a shelf in front of a collection of old ceramic pitchers.

P*umpkin-colored candles in a variety of shapes and sizes fit perfectly into a harvest-themed dining room. Miniature pumpkins, gourds, brightly colored leaves, and baskets of flowers give the entire room a feeling of abundance.*

Partridges, or doves, and pear trees, or just pears, are featured in a refreshing Christmas decor. Rather than traditional red and green, the room is decorated with warm golds and yellows. In the pretty painted chandelier burn candles decorated in a similar style. To do this yourself, simply wipe standard candles with a rag soaked in gold or any other shade of paint. The process adds both color and texture to the candles.

At moments when the house is not fragrant with the aromas of holiday meals, light scented candles to infuse the air with hints of of winter scents: cranberry, cinnamon, orange, or ginger.

No holiday dining table is ready without a centerpiece that includes candles. Instead of a traditional horn of plenty, try filling a wooden bowl with mounds of a single type of seasonal fruit, such as purple concord grapes, lady apples, or seckel pears. Arrange tapers in polished brass or pewter candlesticks and set them next to the bowl, or, if the bowl is flat enough, put pillars of different sizes among the fruit.

Don't forget to decorate the chandelier above the table. Hang glass votive holders from the arms of an electric chandelier or place amber-colored beeswax candles in a nonelectric one. Cradle bittersweet vines in the chandelier's arms.

Envelop your guests in candlelight from the time they arrive. Be lavish in your use of candles throughout the home in the spirit of this holiday.

CHRISTMAS

Candles have long played a central role in the celebration of Christmas. The candle symbolizes the star that led followers to the manger in Bethlehem. In Christian homes throughout the world, some sort of

Christmas candle tradition exists, and most churches feature candles in their Christmas Eve services. The four Sundays before Christmas, known as Advent, are celebrated with a wreath and four candles, or a large Advent pillar candle that is burned each day from Advent Sunday until Christmas, in the final week of the month. The Swedish holiday of St. Lucia's Day on December 13th also features a symbolic wreath, but with five candles instead of four.

Long before Christ, evergreen trees, wreaths, and garlands were symbols of eternal life in many cultures. Early Europeans decorated their houses with pine boughs and candles at the New Year to chase away the devil. Germans began to decorate evergreen trees with candles in the 16th century, and Prince Albert, Queen Victoria's German consort, brought the tradition to England three hundred years later. The bright, candlelit Christmas trees became wildly popular, and the idea quickly made its way to America. Electricity and safety concerns have consigned evergreens festooned with candles to tables and mantels.

A traditional Christmas dining room (OPPOSITE) can be given an extra special feel with candles. Nestled among the evergreens and the covered crystal dishes filled with red Christmas balls are a score of votive candles. Warm a winter sill by planting a candle in a terra-cotta pot (ABOVE) and displaying it with other pots filled with dried herbs, flowers, and ivy.

Celebrate Christmas Eve dinner with a lavishly laid-out table and a little present on every plate. Ribbons and tiny kumquats decorate the packages. Bowls filled with oranges, traditionally put in the toes of Christmas stockings as an out-of-season treat, pick up the theme, and candles with citrus scents will extend it even further. Painted flowerpots hold candles at each end of the table.

HOLIDAY CANDLES

✲

Combining seasonal fruits and vegetables with candles creates an appropriate decorative touch for many holiday celebrations.

✲ **CORE** large apples and use them as holders for tapers. Take a thin slice off the bottom to stabilize the fruit, if necessary.

✲ **GILD** pears, apples, pomegranates, and a pineapple with gold paint. Center the pineapple on a tray, and arrange the other fruit around it. Set a taper securely in the crown of the pineapple and arrange votives among the other fruit around the base. Fill in the arrangement with white flowers or evergreen boughs.

✲ **HOLLOW** out globe artichokes and spray them with silver or gold paint. Place votive candles inside, and arrange them in the center of a holiday table.

✲ **DON'T** abandon pumpkins after Halloween. Make luminarias out of winter squash for Thanksgiving.

ron hog scraper candlesticks of different heights create a vertical arrangement around a tiered cake stand embellished with winter greens, citrus fruits, and nuts. The hog scraper candlestick is so-called because of its resemblance to a tool used in 19th-century rural America to scrape the bristles off hides.

Ways to use candles for Christmas decorating are infinite. Be dramatic and mix dazzling pillars in gold or silver with poinsettias and potted evergreens. Or be subtle and place a candle on a silver tray decorated with holly boughs and surrounded by cherished family tree ornaments.

Don't forget that little touches with candles can really imbue your home with holiday spirit. Place scented votives in glass cups in powder rooms and hallways, and drape strings of popcorn and dried cranberries from chandeliers and sconces. Place a single candle in each window and light them every evening.

NEW YEAR'S

As the winter holiday season climaxes, we look to New Year's Eve for one last, grand celebration. Though there may be no Christmas tree as focal point, the festivities are still marked with the sparkle of holiday silver and crystal. Still, it is a charming idea to feature candles in this most renewing of celebrations. Plan to have a separate set of fresh, white candles at the ready when the clock strikes midnight. Whether you celebrate by yourself, at an intimate dinner for two, or with a gathering of family and friends, toast the glittering promise of the coming year by lighting the new candles precisely at the turn of the year. If you have a large group, everyone can be given an individual candle and a packet of matches, so the candles will be lit simultaneously. Make a simple toast to health and good fortune to mark the future. Have holders set out about the room so the candles can be safely rested once the happy ceremony has concluded.

*A*n unusual chandelier that features thick pillars for light (OPPOSITE) *is festooned simply with evergreen boughs and red beads. Two handsome lanterns light the table. The mirror, decorated casually with pine boughs, doubles the effect of the candlelight.*

Nothing is more elegant than the simplicity of silver candle-holders, here filled with plain white tapers illuminating two unadorned topiary Christmas trees planted in silver bowls (ABOVE).

T*he evergreen tree is one of the most popular symbols of Christmas. Originally the Christmas tree boasted scores of real candles. Although we use electric lights to decorate today's trees, those lights mimic soft candlelight. The Christmas tree holds the place of honor in the bay window of this Victorian living room. Clusters of pillar candles give off a warm glow from the cocktail table, while votive candles are grouped on trays on tables and in the bottom of the armoire. Crystal chandelier drops, an unusual decorative silver ball, mercury glass vases, and crystal liqueur glasses reflect the candlelight to create a scintillating, festive look.*

NEW YEAR'S EVE CANDLES

✻

Candles are absolutely mandatory for New Year's Eve. Here are a few special ideas to create a burst of happy light to bring in the new year:

✻ **MASS** dozens of glass votive candles in even rows or a spiral on top of a mirrored surface or in a silver tray. Add several silver and gold Christmas balls to make the arrangement sparkle.

✻ **BREAK** out all your silver: candlesticks, candelabras, serving bowls, creamers, pitchers, and trays. Polish the silver until it gleams, then put white, silver, or gold tapers, pillars, or votives inside—or on top of—every piece.

✻ **MARK** the holiday with an anniversary candle, one that has each year indicated in increments on its side. Be sure to burn only the numerals for the current year, then store the candle until the next New Year's party.

Chubby pear-shaped candles are almost too pretty to burn. Here the candles accompany pinecones, evergreen boughs, and a moss-covered urn full of paperwhites to create an elegant yet cozy display for a holiday party.

MORE HOLIDAYS IN WINTER

Candles figure prominently in winter holidays throughout the world. The universally celebrated winter solstice, which falls on December 21st, is the shortest day of the year.

In America, where groups from great and tiny lands have come to seek a better life, hundreds of religious observances take place at this time.

The Jewish community, for instance, observes Hanukkah, the Festival of Lights. For eight nights, they celebrate the miracle that followed the Maccabean War, when the temple's one-day supply of lamp oil burned for eight days and nights. A symbol of Hanukkah, the menorah holds eight candles, one for each day of

Randomly placed, candles glow from within the metal grate of a fireplace. Bear in mind that this lovely, informal look is suitable only for a virtually no-traffic area—one without sweeping hems, small children, or curious pets. Atop the mantel, egg-shaped white candles mingle with herb topiaries and cut lilies.

the miracle, with a servant (shammash) candle, which is used to light the others.

Hindus celebrate Diwali, garland of lights, by making sure that no dark corner, whether in the home, shop, or temple, goes unlit.

Beginning each year on the 26th of December, the seven-day harvest festival of Kwanzaa is celebrated by the African-American community. On that day, family members gather to light the first of the multi-colored candles in the kinara, a seven-branched wooden candelabrum. Three red candles symbolize struggle; three green candles embody hopes and dreams; and the single black candle that is placed in the middle of the kinara stands for the pride of the African-American people.

A GIFT OF CANDLES

✳

Present candles creatively, tied with ribbons or grouped in gift baskets.

✤ **PERSONALIZE** the selection. Choose candle scents appropriate to the recipient: invigorating eucalyptus for an athlete or soothing rose for a busy working mother. Combine candles with bath salts, luxurious soap, or a bath pillow.

✤ **STENCIL** a design, such as moons and stars, colored stripes, or an ornate monogram, on the candle with spray paint.

✤ **CARVE** the person's initials into a candle. Trace the monogram on a broad pillar candle, then warm the area to soften. Using a sharp knife, carve the design into the wax.

✤ **MAKE** new candles from old. Salvage the candle remnants from an important celebration and melt them down for a commemorative molded candle.

candle basics

Votive candles in various sizes, shapes, and styles gain impact when clustered together (ABOVE). *Pewter candlesticks evoke images of Colonial America and make exquisite holders for classic dipped tapers* (RIGHT).

C ANDLES ARE BASICALLY SIMPLE OBJECTS, composed just as they were centuries ago of wax and a wick. Today, candle wax is either beeswax, paraffin, or a combination of the two together with various other waxes. Before the development of paraffin in the mid-19th century, candles were made from natural substances, usually beeswax and fats from animals and plants. Tallow, which is made from animal

CANDLE SAFETY

✳ **FIT** candles snugly into holders. Candles that are too loose or too tight may tip over.

✳ **KEEP** matches and other debris that can inadvertently flare up out of the candle.

✳ **NEVER** leave candles unattended. If you are too busy to pay attention, place sand or water in the base of the containers.

✳ **KEEP** lighted candles out of reach of children and pets.

✳ **KEEP** candles away from billowy curtains, bed linens, and other flammable fabrics.

✳ **DO NOT** move glass or ceramic holders if the wax is still hot and molten.

✳ **EXTINGUISH** candles that are smoking or have burned down to within 2 inches of the holder or decorations.

A variety of candles in glistening tin holders next to a vintage breadbox and potted paperwhites makes a pretty country kitchen display.

fat, and oil from sperm whales were both very popular for candlemaking in Colonial America. A lovely greenish-blue wax that naturally coats bayberries was also common. For various reasons, these substances are not widely used today, although for special candles small percentages of animal fat and bayberry wax are sometimes added to beeswax or paraffin.

Paraffin, a by-product of refined oil, is the primary ingredient found in most commercial candles today. Although it is not as supple as beeswax, it is colorless, odorless, and takes color well.

Beeswax, a natural substance secreted by honeybees, remains popular for candlemaking. It is sweet-smelling, long-burning, and tends not to drip as readily as paraffin and other waxes,

C andles and flower arrangements were made for each other, whether in a lavish bouquet at the center of a banquet table flanked by silver candelabras or tiny pots planted with sprigs of dried lavender coupled with a miniature container candle.

but it is expensive. Beeswax is most often sold in sheets, so pure beeswax candles are rolled rather than dipped or molded. Because beeswax is so flexible, it can often be rolled without being warmed first.

Beeswax and other waxy substances including tallow can be added to paraffin to make what connoisseurs call dip-and-carve wax, which is amenable to molding and carving.

Wicks come in three types: flat braid, square braid, and wire-cored, which has a wire center and is generally found in container candles, votives, and floating candles. The size and style of the wick are important measures of the quality of a candle, because they affect how well a candle flames.

CANDLE CARE

✺

✺ **STORE** candles in a cool, dry, dark place. Make sure they are laid flat in a drawer or box to prevent warping.

✺ **CLEAN** dusty or dirty tapers or pillars by wiping them with a clean fine cloth, such as nylon. (An old stocking works well.) If the candles seem a bit dry, wipe them down with a little vegetable oil.

✺ **CARVE** away enough wax with a sharp paring knife to expose the fresh wick if a wick becomes too short to light. Shave a quarter inch of the wax off the top of the candle so the wick will be exposed to the air. Gently shape and smooth the cut edges of the candle with the heat of another flame.

✺ **REFRIGERATE** or freeze candles before using them to make them burn more slowly and evenly.

✺ **AVOID** exposing decorative candles to direct sunlight or hot lamps for long periods of time. Spotlights can cause candles to melt.

General Candle Tips

✺ **TRIM WICKS**. Keep wicks trimmed to about a quarter-inch long and make sure they are straight. A long or crooked wick will cause the candle to burn unevenly, drip, and smoke, while a wick that is too short will drown in wax.

✺ **AVOID DRAFTS**. Never position lit candles in front of an open door or window, a fan, an air conditioner, or any other strong draft. In addition to the fire risk, the air can cause wax to drip and soot to collect, and result in glass containers cracking.

✺ **USE BOBECHES**. To prevent wax from dripping off a chandelier or other candleholders, insert bobeches, glass or metal rims that sit at the base of candles to catch hot wax.

✺ **SHAPE ENDS**. If candles are too large for their holders, trim the ends with a sharp knife; if they are too small, anchor them with sticky wax.

✺ **EXTINGUISH GENTLY**. To avoid splashing wax or a ribbon of smoke, shield the flame and blow lightly, or use a snuffer.

Although candles come in only three types, they can be molded and displayed in a variety of ways. An interesting collection of vases and bowls creates an attractive arrangement of chunky pillars and a single taper.

TYPES OF CANDLES

All candles are either dipped, rolled, or poured. Dipped candles are created by repeatedly dipping wicks into molten wax, and then hanging them to dry and harden. This was the standard method of candle-making until the introduction of paraffin. Gravity naturally pulls the wax down to form more thickly at the base than at the top, resulting in the classic tapered shape. Dipped candles are available in many sizes, but usually vary in length from six to eighteen inches. Rolled candles are made by wrapping flat sheets of wax around wicks.

Molded candles can be found in an infinite variety of shapes, from flowers and animals to figures or buildings. The most familiar molded candle is the

REMOVING WAX

✳

Despite precautions, candle wax can drip on tablecloths and tables, and build up on candleholders. Here's how to remove it:

✳ **FABRIC.** Allow the wax to harden. With a dull knife, gently scrape off the wax. If oil and wax remain, use a sponge to clean the spot with dry-cleaning solvent. Then place the fabric between two paper towels and, using a warm iron, press until no oil appears on the paper towel. Launder as usual.

✳ **WOOD.** Wait until the wax hardens or hold an ice cube against the spilled wax. Scrape off the hard wax with a kitchen spatula, a dull knife, or a plastic credit card. Oil with furniture polish.

✳ **GLASS, PORCELAIN, OR METAL HOLDERS.** Soften the wax by soaking the holders in warm water then gently rub the wax off. For stubborn coatings, freeze the candlestick, then pop the frozen wax out or pick it off the surface. (Avoid using the freezing method when cleaning fragile pieces).

C *lassic tapered candles always look elegant, especially in beautiful silver candlesticks. With the creative use of a color like pale blue and the reflection in a mirror, a traditional decorating technique can take on a more informal look.*

votive. Traditionally, unscented white versions are employed for religious ceremonies; however, votive candles are also available in many colors and fragrances, and so are suitable for virtually any style of decoration.

The chunky pillar is another popular molded style. Pillars can range from a few inches tall to massive church candles that can be as tall as four or five feet. Large molded candles, some more than twelve inches in diameter, are often formed with multiple wicks. Recently, square and block candles, also with multiple wicks, have appeared on the market.

CANDLEHOLDERS

Candlesticks have been the basic holders for candles for thousands of years. In Colonial times, only the wealthy owned candlesticks made of silver,

pewter, or crystal, and everyday holders tended to be made of tin, wood, or cruder blown glass.

Like the candles themselves, candlesticks can be combined and arranged in many ways. Unmatched candlesticks can be pulled together with candles of the same type (tapers, perhaps) or color (pastels or bright Christmas red.) Decorative styles and periods can be blended with candlesticks. For example, wrought-iron folk art candleholders are stunning arranged on a stark contemporary glass dining table.

In French, the word *chandelier* means simply "candlestick," but we use it to describe an elaborate style of candleholder, a fixture that holds multiple lights and usually hangs from the ceiling. Today, most chandeliers are electrified, but small, old-fashioned styles that hold candles are available and make charming decorative devices, especially in an intimate space.

The word sconce comes from the Old French word *esconce*, which meant "lantern" or "hiding place," and refers to a wall lamp. Until the late 17th century, the sconce was the most common tool for lighting a room, after the illumination thrown by the fireplace. Sconces are often backed with a shiny material such as brass, copper, or silver to reflect and maximize the candle's illumination. Often, too, a sconce will include a glass lantern to protect the flame from drafts.

C *andleholders offer great possibilities for decorating. Three pillar candles are placed in quite different styles of candleholder* (ABOVE). *The similar size and color of the candles, together with the antiqued finish on the candleholders, unifies the arrangement. In a corner cupboard, several stubby pillars inside milky goblets and bowls create a luminous display* (LEFT).

Votive candles can be as charming as they are useful. Plain white votives set in chic ultra-modern holders are placed on a shelf of collectibles to illuminate the surrounding area and highlight artistic prints.

CONTAINER CANDLES

✺

Container candles are very easy to make and are marvelous gifts. Try these ideas:

✺ **UNMATCHED** sugar bowls and creamers, especially odd-lot silver ones, and porcelain tea cups.

✺ **BABY CUPS**, silver christening mugs, or children's drinking glasses to give to kids, new mothers, or the original owner, perhaps as a graduation present.

✺ **FOR EASTER**, eggshells, perhaps painted decoratively, as mini-candleholders when set in eggcups.

In their amazing array of colors, candles provide a relatively inexpensive yet luxurious way to enhance any color scheme. This lovely lavender taper makes an appealing vision, especially when combined with fresh pink flowers.

MAKING CANDLES AT HOME

Crafting simple candles in molds or containers at home is quite easy. Most hobby stores carry paraffin wax, molds, and other supplies. Softer wax generally requires a thicker wick while harder wax works better with a thinner wick. Beeswax is viscous and therefore needs a thicker wick than the same-sized paraffin candle.

Make sure the candle container is clean and dry. Follow the manufacturer's instructions for melting the wax. Pour hot wax into the container, and allow it to semi-set. Gently insert a wire-core wick, then let the candle harden completely. Setting times will vary depending upon the size of the candle. Trim the wick to a quarter inch before lighting.

index